Bord for En

Bord for En*

(*Swedish for "Table for One")

Poems

David Holper

BROKEN TRIBE PRESS

Bord för En
Copyright © 2025 David Holper

First Edition

Paperback ISBN: 9781965412268

Cover art by John Wesa

Cover design by Jacob Arms
Published by Broken Tribe Press
Lawrence Landing Company
Raleigh, North Carolina 27609
USA, North America
www.brokentribepress.com

Broken Tribe Press is a proud member of:

Independent Book Publishers Association
 and
Community of Literary Magazines and Presses

BROKEN TRIBE PRESS

Advance Praise for *Bord for En*

"Beginning in our confinement via Covid circa 2020, the poems in David Holper's beautiful book aver that the lessons of solitude prove the door to outside is any one that you open. Bord för En takes readers on a pilgrimage, our pilgrim-poet navigating through the enforced interior of a pandemic to arrive at the real locale of human solitude, wherein the pain of the past is brought to task and that pain, while not gone, is diminished. The physical effort I felt in reading these poems, especially those dedicated to hiking, seemed as tactile and true as the stations-of-the-cross."

—Claudia Keelan, author of *We Step into the Sea: New and Selected Poems*

"I am learning to bear / this terrible miracle of stones," writes David Holper in *Bord för En*, his latest collection of poems. These poems are full of miracles—hiking through Northern California's Headwaters Forest, reflecting elegiacally on a fraught relationship with his father, and navigating the emotional terrain of the Covid-19 pandemic. But this is no mere pandemic chronicle. Holper's work invites us into a larger meditation on resilience, grief, and wonder. "Be teachable," he urges, "until you draw your last breath." *Bord för En* is a poignant, lyrical waypoint on that lifelong journey.

—Sandra Simonds, author of *Assia*

"*Tikkun olam* is Jewish spiritual practice of 'world repair,' poet David Holper tells us, and that phrase could serve as the title for this book, because there is really no better way of speaking of this holy project. In lucid and clear lyric poems (well-crafted, but never drawing attention to their craft), the poet addresses the world's beauty and describes the hardest sorrows we inflict upon the planet and each other, in order to involve us in the action of repair and to pull us closer to "the hour...when the spirit awakens us / to all that is undone." Moving through landscapes he makes vividly available—whether he's speaking of the Pacific Northwest or Spain—Holper uses his considerable gifts with language to get his readers to where "we are left / in mute witness of our lives at once so brief, so luminous." *Bord för En* is an invitation to a pilgrimage as well as a feast: you will want to take the nourishing and healing journey: 'If this is the only way the world may be mended, / then I say yes...'"

Laura Mullen, author of *EtC*

Bord för En* was a Swedish pop-up restaurant that was opened at the start the pandemic and closed on August 1, 2020. The restaurant was a single table in a field, and the food was sent via a cable in a basket. Only one person per day was served.

CONTENTS

I.

Bord för En   1
Uncertainty   2
Zoonotic Spillover   3
Berlin   4
Socotra   5
The Luxury of Hope   6
The Way Back   8
Destination   9

II.

Hiking the New Year   13
Seven Silences   15
Meditation Descending...   18
Klamath River Blessing   20
Three-mile Bridge, Late Summer...   21
Hiking to Hyperion   22
Circumnavigating Mt. Tamalpais...   24
Meseta   27

III

All That You Will Never Know   31
Dear Past   32
Flavors of Fear   33
Superpower   34
Chernobyl Spring   36
Roadside Grave   38
Accident   40
Cruz de Ferro   41

IV

Working Within a Form	45
Pairing	46
Subjunctive Mood	47
Aubergine	48
The Tunnel	49
Abcedarian on the Cusp of Despair	51
Blood Necessity	52
North Jetty	54

V

Karaoke Bar	57
Poetry Is Not a Horserace	58
On Reading My Name in the...	59
A Different Clock	60
Epithalamium	61
Crush	63
Based on a True Story	65
Slam	67

VI

America Is Not a Racist Country*	73
April Fools	75
Another Shark	76
Connecting the Dots	78
Goodbye, Ancient Friends	80
Just Maybe,	81
Silences	82
Tikkun Olam	83

VII

Master Class in Disaster   87
Ordinary Miracle   89
The Secret of Poetry   92
Invitation   93
Meditation on Approaching the...   94
This Sacred Task   95
First Farmers Market After the...   97
The Earthquake   98

Acknowledgements   103

Dedicated to the millions of people who died of Covid-19, their loved ones and friends who still bear those losses, the health care workers who cared for those patients, and all those who continue to struggle with the effects of Covid-19.

"In my recurring dream, I'm in a play
but I don't seem to know my lines,
and I can never find the script,
but when my curtain call comes,
I want to know I was someone who found a way
to just let go of all that shit."

—Antje Duvekot "Dylan Thomas"

"What cannot be said will be wept."

—Sappho

I

Bord för En*

Please sit. Notice how your table holds the earth,
so you may find your feet. Notice how like the
flightless cormorant hidden in the Galapagos for
centuries, it stands apart.

In this spirit, we have cooked up something special
today—safety. It pairs with a lapis lazuli side
of sky, over a russet bed

of this fallow field. We promise we will leave you
utterly alone. We will winch over your meal via cable
in a wicker basket. We drape

a little cloth over the food, a checkered history
like the print from Dorothy's dress in which the
tornado swept her far from monochrome plains

of before. What else is available?
Sorry, we're out of assurances.
Still, in this maelstrom, rest assured,

it remains the safest restaurant in the world.
If when your food arrives, a sparrow alights,
we would appreciate it if you offer her

a little bread, some water from your glass. She has come
so far to be with you—and it takes so little to show you
have not left your manners—or humanity at home.

Uncertainty

That spring when the disease spread
like storm clouds we all sat in the darkness
of our homes, baking, or eating, or peering out over
the internet, wondering when the light would return.
We fumbled our messages: "stay safe" or "be well."
The number one song in America was "Say So."
No one could say anything certain about the future.
In that darkness, no one could tell what would happen
when the country reopened, like some intricate
Chinese puzzle. Who, after all, knew whether schools
would be face-to-face in the fall or if students all over
America would once again stare like zombies zooming
into their computer screens, wondering if this was the
best that the future had to offer? No one knew if there
would ever be a vaccine, no matter the hundreds of
efforts underway, or if six feet would always be the
distance, or the depth. Even with our loved ones, if
someone fell sick in the darkness, the best we could do
was to wall them off from us, praying the virus would
stay put. The mathematical modelling was vague.
The testing, insufficient. The leadership? A bad joke.
The only sure thing anyone was counting on was
hope, that beautiful, feathered thing that seemed to
have flown the coop as we sat in our homes making
avatars of ourselves for no purpose whatsoever.

Zoonotic Spillover*

The body is a house: alone, weathered,
perched on a promontory. Although it's spring,
and the winds are howling in off the sea,
the doors and windows have been thrown wide open:
the lace curtains waving desperately. If someone
were to wander out to the where the house stands,
nothing would stop them from barging in.
They could invite their friends. They could
bring bats. They might throw a party,
and by the time you discover the wreckage
they have left, it might leave you gasping
for breath, feverous with rage. Go inside now.
Fasten the windows. Lock the doors.
Take a breath. Tell yourself everything
is going to be okay,
even if you understand it isn't.

* According to Plowright et al., a "**zoonotic spillover**"
is defined as the "transmission of a pathogen from a
vertebrate animal to a human."

Berlin

My mother's family fled Berlin in 1937
just before the borders slammed shut,
caging the other Jews and anyone else the Nazis found
disposable. I visited the city several times
while the wall still stood. Every time
I found myself in the city of bears,
I pictured my grandmother's stories of the delights of
the theater, the white asparagus wrapped in ham,
their wonderful apartment—
images in a faded photograph.
This late spring news arrives of a Bolivian pan flute
orchestra trapped at Rheinsberg Palace, unable to take
flight, unable to do anything but practice six hours
every day. They are permitted to wander as far as the
forest line on the 600-acre property.
Wolves prowl beyond. Every time I imagine
them there, I think of my grandfather Daniel and his
brother driving back to Berlin from a porcelain factory
they owned. Stuck behind a slow-moving truck,
they couldn't endure the glacial crawl, so they veered
onto the shoulder, racing to save mere minutes.
They plowed into tree—and my grandfather died at the
crash while his brother survived until the next day.
What does this have to do with borders or orchestras
or the pandemic? Nothing, I imagine.
It is only where my mind travels in the long hours
of solitude. Out beyond any walls, along the forest line
where the wolves dwell. In the midst of memory
and dreams, wondering what the future
has waiting for us in the dark forest ahead.

Socotra

She walks with an enormous
emptiness: a great wildness
she is learning to live with. See it

in her elusive smile beneath the dragon blood tree,
or in the sweep of her red skirt at the cliff's edge,
as if to say, here I am—opening myself

to the emptiness. At night she sleeps
in the billion-star hotel; by day she feeds
a fire on the beach and bends to its fragrant warmth.

When she puts out to sea in her boat, she notices
depths greater than she has ever fathomed. The hours
understand her: the days no longer

interrupt. You may wonder how
she endures such solitude: This is the lesson
where the self you inhabit is at best

an emptying shell: this older,
deeper self abides,
inviting you to awaken.

When the pandemic began, Polish *YouTube* travel
vlogger Eva zu Beck was stranded on Socotra, a sparsely
populated desert island in the Indian Ocean. She spent three
months there before finding passage home on a freighter.

The Luxury of Hope

We comb the beach on this last day of the year,
threading the tideline. We eye the jagged edge
of the flotsam: carefully, we scramble over rock

and mud, ford streams, study the remnant.
We split up, two heading north to Little River,
two going south to the hazy end of Clam Beach.

The sun breaks through, offering its late December
failings while the sea growls darkly in its explosive
midnight blue curlings. A flock of pelicans

floats leisurely outside the wave break eyeing us.
Where the beach yields to sea, we trudge back north
in silence. We find nothing, find ourselves teetering

between hope and despair: the day before we'd learned
our friend's son ventured out into the wilderness
of the Pacific in a canoe

—and didn't return. This first day of searching
we offer ourselves the freedom to imagine
scenarios where he might have landed safely

on a sea stack, his canoe borne away;
or maybe the canoe was swamped, but he floated
safely ashore. Neither of us say what we fear,

though it shadows us all afternoon. We meet
our daughters back at the car, share empty news.
We bear this bright façade through the long last night

of this terrible year. No one need tell us what is coming.
We understand well enough someone
will find the shattered canoe, but for now, we raise

our glasses and toast, ushering out the old
year, tonguing every bittersweet drop
of this offering, this luxury of hope.

The Way Back

I slipped out under cover of darkness to breathe
in the autumnal chill. Darkness went before me;
and it followed, like a ravenous wolf, sniffing my steps.
Who made me, I wondered. What hand would willingly
throw me into the world, a place of such enormous
suffering, such terrifying beauty?
I descended under the soft green darkness
of the redwoods, until I found myself alone
at the pond, where the moon bent down and distilled
itself on the mirror-like surface. The ducks tucked
their heads under their downy wings and slept,
dreamless. I had no answers for the malignant
shadow within, nor beyond. All I could do was ask and
wait. The pond smelled of weeping willows. An owl
hooted, launching itself into air, searching for its next
kill. The blood moon froze, watching from the blasted
crowns of the redwoods, unable to be other than itself.
And I—I resolved to discover what I was made for,
chasing the darkness back, so I might unpack my soul.
If ever I finish, I will forge a new way back, making
peace with the dying world as it is, and myself within.

Destination

After the dead have left us, where do they go?
Is it merely into the moldering earth
where we place them, that they go?

Is it to heaven or hell, that they escape
the bounds of this earth,
or do they dissolve like sugar into the stars as they go?

No one who claims they can explain, has an explanation
that will serve. When they say, I know
where the dead go,

you can ask them, have you been there? Have you died
and passed over and back, so you can say with certainty
where the dead go.

And no sacred text or dogma offers us
what anyone knows when they see their loved ones go.

Perhaps if God himself speaks to you, she might whisper
in your ear this simple secret, and tell you, beloved,
where you are going too.

II

Hiking the New Year

The wind brings the smell of rain—and more
rain. I celebrate by lacing up my boots. I begin

with the hills in the park nearby, legs burning
from doing nothing all fall. Days later

I hike out to Headwaters, find myself soaked
in sweat and struggling to catch my breath

trudging up the two-mile hill above three-mile bridge.
Yesterday, I hiked out to Fern Canyon, almost nine

miles out and back under a gray sky. I walked alone,
only a Chestnut-backed Chickadee's song to shape

the silence of the redwoods. She reminds me of the
girls in my high school choir, the ones who seemed

almost invisible with their plain faces, their dowdy
clothes, until they began to sing—and you'd discover

you knew nothing about them. Until then,
at most you saw was your own reflection

on the surface of the waters. I don't know where a single
one of them lives now, or what they do, or who loves

them, but walking into the mist gradually dissolving
into rain, I hope they still sing—in the shower, at a

coffee shop, in another choir. Opening their mouths
and awakening us all to our blindness:

this foolish assumption we already understood
the universe and our pale sphere within it.

Seven Silences

I)

Deep in the woods on the way to Headwaters Forest,
you struggle to push aside the clot of worry. A hermit
thrush throats its plaintive cry. Then.
Only the hush
of breath.

II)

You hear an old friend contracts Covid in NYC.
You call a friend of a friend for her number, which
you've lost. Somehow you get through. The phone
cannot stop ringing, even after you hang up.

III)

On the way back from Emerald Creek
you turn an ankle climbing the long ascent
to the prairie. In the last steep mile,
you ask yourself, what is there to be afraid
of in the dark?

IV)

A nightmare. Shaking,
waking, you list all the people
you have loved,
or should have
who have
left.

V)

Standing atop
Wedding Rock
looking south.
Only the distance speaks:
a faint punctuation
where rock abrades itself,
trying to embrace the always
arriving
wave.

VI)

You find an old photo of your dead father
when he was a boy in Shanghai.
On his right shoulder
a black blur hovers.

You want to ask him
what that uncertain shadow means,
but he remains
stubbornly
silent.

VII)

The winter silences
any thoughts of peace — atmospheric rivers
trying to blow down
the house.

Days later only sunshine:
the slow drip of retreat
from the eaves. In each droplet,
sunlight summons a tiny rainbow

so quiet, you can almost
hear each color whisper
its essential secret.

Meditation Descending Dolason Prairie

Let us say the ancients were right—that the self breeds
a set of fictions founded upon sand. That walking alone

in winter in the woods with my thoughts is akin to a
mass of mosquitoes buzzing in a monotonous cloud—

not so much reality as it is a misty mirror in which to
imagine the self as familiar. I had a lover once who after

her passion undid her whispered to me, see—there was
not even skin between us. Perhaps it was a joke. Perhaps

at such a moment, our souls wind a tightwire to walk
into the abyss of another. I tramp on past the remains

of the old sheep barn, across the meadow, leaved with
madrones and bays. In that shade, my thoughts unravel.

Only my body beats the rhythm of my steps. I let slip my
memories; I let slip hands, feet, body, bones. I cross

another prairie, disappearing into the deeper shadows of
the sentinel redwoods. I catch my breath at the bridge

crossing Emerald Creek, then top the ridge to descend
into the darkening shadows of the Tall Trees Grove.

At Redwood Creek, I sit by the water's edge, almost
forgetting my purpose. I pluck a piece of white chert

from the waters—weigh the gritty shape of this body—
ready to pocket it. My error reveals itself: I set the stone

back to be worn away to nothing—ready to go on,
unsuited, but ready, nonetheless.

Klamath River Blessing

Let the waters of the Klamath be released.
Let the walls of the four hydroelectric dams be blasted
apart, ripped down to bedrock,
      concrete and rebar pulverized so only the scars
will testify to what once spoiled the river.
Let the rains come and wash away the remains—
the silt, the pesticides, the cyanobacteria
—all the old hatreds, the blood of genocide
      until the waters sweep away the past;
Let the waters, the mighty waters sweep down from the
headwaters through Ishi Pishi Falls, carrying away the
foulness spilling out past Requa and the Klamath Bar
      until the living and the dead gather for the story
of a river reborn; Then let all that still swims return
—the Coho, the Chinook,
      the ancient Green Sturgeon,
      the Lost River and short-nosed suckers;
Let them leap and fight their way upriver to clean
gravel beds where the hens may rest their sacred eggs
amidst the stones,
      so the jacks may pass their blessing over this
new generation; And later when the offspring have
returned, let us all gather to feast—the heron, coyote,
the eagle and osprey, the brown bear, the Yurok, the
Hupa, the Karuk—all who still hunger for rebirth; Yes,
let the waters of the Klamath run wild once again and
      bowing to the dead, let all the world be renewed.

The final removal of the Klamath River dams was completed
in October 2024. The process involved the removal of four
hydroelectric dams: Copco No. 2, Copco No. 1, Iron Gate, and
J.C. Boyle. It was the largest dam removal in US history.

Three-mile Bridge, Late Summer, Headwaters

At the railing, listen to all that is offered: the song
of the creek below, a glass of water
poured endlessly over cobble. The lonely song

of a hermit thrush, somewhere unseen, a reminder
of so much just beyond perception.
High above, a gentle wind stirs the canopy like a sigh.

Summer grows short. My daughter will leave
for the city soon. A sycamore leaf drops in slow
motion from above, landing in the water spinning—
and is slowly borne away.

Hiking to Hyperion

Just after the summer solstice, I hike to see
Hyperion, the tallest tree in the world.
I come thinking, I suppose, of myself:
of the story I will tell or the photos
I will share. Hiking up the creek
though, I lose myself in the cold clear
water, the lazy scooting of the frogs
from before my feet. The light grows
green and washes away whatever foolish ideas
or worries I had borne with me. I climb
over and under the fallen redwoods
along the creek, balancing on the moss-
covered way, careful to keep my footing,
careful to do no harm. I lose my breath,
I lose my way, wandering up a false trail,
thinking I have arrived. I resign myself
to failure. I cross over one more
fallen tree where the way opens
like an abracadabra. I ascend
the hill where the ancient giant stands.
At its base, you cannot see how towering
the tree really is—just as well.
It is just a giant among other giants,
but it is enough to show how small a thing I am.
I stand there a great while, thinking
of the centuries this tree has stood,
thinking of how it will stand long after
I am gone. I breath in the lush air the forest
offers. Then I silently give thanks to be
in the presence of such a being

before I hike back to my truck
and climb into the self
that so easily forgets
such vastly important
things.

Circumnavigating Mount Tamalpais with My Daughter, October 9, 2021

"... circling and climbing—chanting—to show respect and to clarify the mind." —Gary Snyder

Up out of the half light of the morning, we fit our feet
into the footsteps of those who have gone before us.
We rise through redwoods and sword ferns, bay and
madrone, huckleberry and manzanita on this blue
October morning. If there is a name for the thin places
of the world, it is this.

Selah

Up the steep grade, we chuff like bears
until the way eases, and we arrive at Pan Toll.
We push on disappearing into the golden prairie grass,
walking up through the dry oaks and madrones, looking
on the center of the world, the serpentine infusion,
like a ship's prow, parting the fog of millennia.

Selah

We lose the trail briefly above the mountain theater, re-
find our way up the folds of the mountain and down into
the solitude of the forest as if crossing over into
something neither of us know the name for.
The mountain grows drier in the rain shadow, all scrub
and rock and sun, and I warn my daughter who is taking
the lead, *Watch out for rattlesnakes basking in the
sunshine.* It's a long, quiet walk in the shadows of the

trees, and there is only the whisper of breath and the tap
of our poles on the trail rock, the red bark and leaf fall
from the madrones: a cinnamon-colored sweetness in
the shade.

Selah

Then the last struggle up the steepest section:
When we arrive at east peak and the stark emptiness of
the fire lookout, the whole of the Bay and Pacific, hills
and valleys, cities and towns opens below us. In the
bright blue of the day, we imagine we can see forever—as
far as Point Reyes and Drakes Beach to the west, Mt. St.
Helena to the north, Mt. Diablo to the east, and coastline
to the south of the Golden Gate, stretching away
into the southern distance. We stretch under the sky
and receive the sun's blessings on the warm rocks.

Selah

Snyder's words about smog come back to me, but the
world has sickened more than he might have guessed,
greenhouse gasses warming the planet, unleashing
droughts, fires, and fire tornadoes more terrible than
imagination. Lakes and rivers drying up, storms more
ferocious than any preparation. What a fragile web we
have built for ourselves over these 10,000 years
of civilization and how easily it unravels. I do not say
any of this to my daughter who stretches out
on sun-warmed rock, a raven waiting patiently
by her feet for a morsel from her hand.
She already knows.

Selah

As if falling, we descend in the heat of the afternoon, dropping from the east peak down the steps of Fern Creek, into the cool canopy until it tees into Old Railroad Grade. We head east to what remains of the Hogback. Finally, we arrive at Mountain Home, cross the road, find the Canopy Trail and descend into the musty fecund stillness of the redwoods. The last few miles we trudge, our bodies spent but still, there is a numinous glow in both of us, celebrating the miles we have walked with one another, celebrating the mountain and its ancient patience, celebrating how thin this veil between us—between everything.

Selah

(Note: quote is from Gary Snyder's poem "The Circumambulation of Mt. Tamalpais')

Meseta*

The emptiness jackets the land, clasps the sky, which
is too big for any camera, too vast even for words.

I trudge with the others in the silence, and the silence
mends into us. The only sounds are the crunch of

gravel below our boots, the click of our walking poles
with each swing. When the heat sets July on fire, in

darkness I set out alone with a headlamp as my only
guide. After the moon curtsies at the horizon, sunrises

bloom into a daily epiphany brushed in pink, purple,
umber, lapis lazuli. The light washes through the

wheatfields and cobblestone streets of the pueblos,
which sit illuminated upon a hill, overseeing the

distances. The yellow arrows wind to a plaza, a church,
or cathedral. There in the afternoons I sit in the shade

of an umbrella drinking *tinto de verano* to wash down
the dust. Later, there'll be time for the pilgrim's mass.

When the wafer is laid on my tongue, the goblet of wine
lifted to my lips, I confess the same longing for which

words fail. Yet I ask just the same for this grace: that I
may go on walking out into the great abundance

where my heart cannot help but awaken
to the whispering spirit.

* The meseta is the name given to the large and expansive flat plains of central Spain.

III

All That You Will Never Know

The names of all the stars. The names
of everyone you've ever met. The names
of all the trees. Or the flowers. Or
the birds. Rocket science. The way to stop
your lover's tears, as neatly as handing her
a neatly wrapped gift. The way you
once could. How to paint. How to draw. How
to drive a race car. Or pull a 360. How
to talk to a beautiful stranger at a party. Why
lithium flattens the roller coaster ride. Calculus.
The name of that bird whose song illuminates the air
every morning when you wake. The name
of that haunting song just beyond memory.
Why you are always so sad.
Why everyone is always so sad
but pretends not. What cures hangovers.
Why capitalism doesn't work. Why religion doesn't
work. Why socialism, communism, dadaism. Why
torture never yields truth. Why when you kiss,
it no longer sends that blue ribbon of magic
under both your skins. Why the full moon hangs like a
doorway you are not allowed enter. Why nothing
explains why the world
is so terribly beautiful—and everyone
you love must die.

Dear Past,

I am sorry I set you down. I had dragged you such
great distances away from those gray rooms & my
father's glass eye still sitting on the table. Away
from the portrait of my mother's absence hanging
there like the echo of the sea in an alphabet cone,
missing the letter M. I am sorry I could not bear the
tangled forest of your sorrows and stranded you there
just outside of the town where the hero had left to find
his father—or perhaps appeared elsewhere as a dark-
eyed stranger. Either way, I cannot remember. That
memory too rests on the roadside gravel, where you
sit listening to the moan of traffic heading into now.

I tell you I am sorry, but of course you understand I
am lying. I am lying about the house, I am lying about
my parents. I am lying about you. I could not wait to
abandon you. I had long had in mind to reinvent
myself, like a wheel or a mechanical bird or the wind,
but all I became was this same self, staring into the
glass, where the future awaits. I suspect the future
is your doppelgänger. No one seems to know or will
offer me the truth. Still, I am not afraid to step beyond
the future's open door. I am certain it is nothing more
than a ticket for a train ride to a country where neither
of you can reside. I will go bearing nothing into that
strange land, as is the custom, but what need is there
for this body in a house where only soul bears the
invitation to the dance?

Flavors of Fear

That dream where you're tumbling headfirst
off the Golden Gate Bridge
and all the water has gone on vacation.

Your strangled voice when they say to you
stand up in front of everyone.

That time when they said, sit down.
Time's up.

In the fall, that dream of wandering the hallways
naked, wondering what it is you're supposed to be
teaching, and the principal taps you
on your naked shoulder.

Being 900 feet up a cliff
when the lightning starts talking.

Noticing how when fall arrives, everything
reminds you of death.

A morning when you're staring at yourself in the
mirror and think:
Move on. There's nothing to see here.

Superpower

Middle school: imagine your parents left you for dead,
while running away from one another. Laying there,

feeling the breath blow out of you like a balloon,
you chose flying. You dreamed that if only you had a

set of white wings on your back, you could transcend
your parents in their separate wastelands, and up

there, unbuckle your sadness and toss it down from
the blue air like offloading a box of anchors.

By high school, when your father remarried, you
chose invisibility, knowing all too well that your

wicked stepmonster was a perfect fit for a grimmer
fairy tale. In that house, you reasoned that if no one

heard you, no one saw you, you could slide like
shrapnel through the days and pick up the pieces as

an adult, one with the legal right to live anywhere
apart from them. Lacking that, you dressed in armor

to keep out the chill of their anger or indifference.
Surprise. It didn't work.

When they threw you out, you lied, said surviving was
a superpower, just crawling out of sheets every

morning, standing in front of the mirror without
being sick at the sight of yourself took every ounce of

courage you lacked. You didn't mean to hate yourself
the way they taught you, but their curses proved

stickier than you thought, trickier to pull off your skin
when it was just you alone in your head with them

explaining the number line and why you would always
fall to the left of zero. Time freezes. They get old. They

both die. You thought, finally, you can just try and be
more positive with yourself, more forgiving of the

damage they seared into your flesh. That works about
as well as a rusted bicycle with no wheels.

One morning you tell the voices in your head,
enough. You've been living rent free up there for too

long. You resolve that the only thing to do is choose a
better superpower, say, love: you know the kind that

pours like warmed syrup over pancakes, the kind that
hugs you hard, says nothing, despite everything you've

done, or neglected to do, and doesn't give a hoot if
you've driven all your friends away; makes no

difference if no one else loves you. With this
superpower, you peel away the layers of dead skin,

poisonous hatreds, and you let it all go, not so much
like that box of anchors, but like the whole damned

sea going back to bed. Standing before the mirror,
your x-ray vision reveals where the first feathers will

sprout, and you sing for what they will make of you.
You sing with perfect pitch, opening your mouth wide,

harmonizing with your better self, wondering what it
will feel like when the wind lifts you above the past,

and love blesses everything from horizon to horizon.

Chernobyl Spring

That April in Hoechst the earth whispered warning. Our sergeant said nothing about the meltdown or the fire. After I asked about the fallout and the fire, he said that we would be training just same as always: six am sharp in the city park across the street from our company office. I didn't bother mentioning to him how the German papers had warned people to stay out of the wet grass in the morning. I didn't mention there was no particle too small that couldn't plant its seed of destruction. We did pushups in that wet grass; we did sit-ups; we ran out two-mile training runs every morning (our breath chuffing in the humid air) while the fireman climbed up on the roof (human robots they called themselves) and soaked in enough radiation that not one of them would live—and every single one would be buried in lead-lined coffins in a cemetery no loved one would be allowed to visit. That same week I read in the newspaper that Germans shouldn't drink milk, but the army kept on serving it just the same, without a word of warning. It was as if the army held some mighty shield that could hold off wind or ash or harm. I drank the milk with my coffee. I did my sit-ups and pushups in the wet grass and ran my two miles every morning, every breath scorching my lungs, knowing full well I was out of my mind for keeping silent, knowing that my silence was the same logic that all soldiers must follow in blind obedience to death.

Roadside Grave

I know it makes no sense, but there is a hill
        leading downward out of the town where I live.
          It doesn't make sense,
                not because there is such a hill

snaking away, but because halfway up the hill stands
        a retaining wall on which someone fixed a
          cross, flowered it in plastic blossoms,
              bouquets, and farewells. Someone

crashed there years ago. It makes no sense
        that for decades now this survivor decorates the
          cross with flowers, as if to say, this place
            of no importance is more

important than any other place they know. It makes
        no sense that love lives on when there is no one
          left to love. But I know in your town,
             you wouldn't have to drive far to find

such a shrine. They are everywhere. And everywhere
        someone decorates them with flowers, knowing
          that their loved one will never come back
           from the grave, knowing it makes no sense

to say I love you, but saying it anyway, day by day,
        year by year, saying into the nothingness, you
          may think forever will wear me down, but
           the truth is, eternity is too short a time
              to conquer such love.

If you doubt me, go for a drive and look for such a
cross. And when you do, give some thought to
who will fit blossoms into your cross, until
forever gives up and calls it a day.

Accident

I didn't see the blade coming. I didn't see
how the fellow on the other end of the misery whip
made the mistake of pushing and how the saw bowed,
stuck, released—and bit the top of my knee, opening
my leg to the artery. Sometimes we don't know
where we stand until something goes wrong:
the tire blows, the engine won't start, someone says
I don't love you anymore. Pain blossoms like a peony,
and the world shrinks to the inconsequential arena
of your suffering. Later, looking back, it's as if a
window were opened, and you stare back at how your
chest opened, someone cut out your heart and held it
up to the critical inquiry of the light. I didn't know
what any of this meant: all I knew was the blood was
bright red and beat to the rhythm of my heart.
Someone tied a tourniquet above the saw cut.
My crew fetched a stretcher and carried me back up
out of the stand of redwoods to our van. I soaked a
box of Kleenex with the blood seeping out of my
damaged knee. Pain calls for our undivided attention,
as if we needed reminding how little time is offered.
The doctor stitched a line of Xs across the divide in
my flesh. Keep it clean, he said. Somehow, I managed
to follow his advice, healed, learned how to forget
whatever lesson was tied to the damage. Only now,
examining the two shark bite scars across my knee do
I finally understand it was no accident to learn how
deep pain must go—this first lesson in all the deeper
woundings to follow.

Cruz de Ferro

I have pulled down the blinds on this bright afternoon
to match my exhaustion. I have worked since I was 15,

which means I have spent almost five decades selling
the days of my life to feed my family & myself.

With the sands running down, I do not want to
squander even a minute more in unhappiness. I do

not want to resent anyone or listen to anyone resent
me. In Spain, high atop a lonely hill, there stands an

iron cross where pilgrims come and lay a stone or
some token at the base: It has grown into a great

mound of stones pilgrims have carried across Spain,
across continents, across every corner of the world.

They drop them to honor someone's suffering or in
remembrance of their dead. As for me, I will bear

my own burden, a stone so heavy it has nearly broken
me. I will let it fall, saying thanks for all that remains.

Here in the shadows of the afternoon my imaginings
are the seeds of that gratitude. Until that luminous

day, I will bear my labors without complaint. Let the
shadows fall far over the afternoon until the evening

can answer. I am finally learning patience. I am
learning to bear this terrible miracle of stones.

IV

Working within a Form

There is a tension in the form
that forms a tension in the line
that speaks to how you choose a word

or cut one free—to simplify.
There is a tension in a life
living within this sense of form

and having it, you work within
what bounds your days
between sun and shade,

making you choose with care
what will and will not suffice.
And thus, you choose

a form and fashion well:
so when you're done,
the scars won't tell.

Pairing

These two dolomite stones bedded together
until the lower one—through wind, weather, and water—

made a bowl of itself for the smaller one in which to fit.
They rest together as if asleep. Together they are

no larger than an egg: stolid, solitary, gritty.
Imagine in that distant waiting, they did not ignore

the rise or fall of tides or even the poking
of an inquisitive crab. For the moment, they sit

in a basket by my sink. I wonder
at them some time in their great patience,

thinking how after I am long worn down
to nothing, they will sit

a little longer and awaken
in their stony quietude.

Subjunctive Mood

If you place the vase

If on the shoulder of a mountain a cabin

If on a dusty shelf where your aged fingers nose,

remembering

If the whiteout of fog rises through the redwoods

like water

If the vase is rough to the touch, but blue to the eye

If the body then is this:

a container holding certain cerulean

If what cannot be said must be said in ways that words

do not nor cannot

If ashes are all the bell-shaped vase still holds

If this vase resting in your hands is where tears must not

If what you could not say to your father

that last dark moment was

If cannot is all that you can manage now

If finally. You place back

If the fog still practices its forgetting

If nothing transforms but you, in setting,

Aubergine

You can tell its ripeness by the deep lush purple
of the skin, the tight, taut feel it has, so you can
depress a finger into its flesh—and they will answer
by welling into your fingerprint. They are clan

of the nightshade family, their darker cousins.
My father used to cook them up
into *baklazhannaya ikra*, poor man's caviar,
and we feasted, knowing no better of the real thing.

How light they are, in hand, after they turn. Much like
the dead, after their spirits have fled. My father's body
only ash in the urn I held in hand. The boat paused,
just near Sausalito, and I gazed out over the waters.

How I hated him, how I had loved him despite his
anger, his scalding wit. How he loved to laugh at
people to show them how little he thought of their
pretenses. If he drank, be prepared, we'd say. If he
smoked, it seemed he'd set the house on fire.

The urn in my hand felt round and black as some
bitter aubergine. Are there any words to forgive such
things? I leaned out and poured those bits of bone
and ash upon the waters, speechless, yes,
but trying my damndest to empty him out of me
forever.

The Tunnel

I cannot tell you how strange and wonderful that
summer was. All I can say for certain is that Paul
claimed the middle class, sleepy suburbs had
hypnotized us stone dead. That explosive summer he

detonated the mundane shells our parents had stuffed
us into: first in some crazy horror film he cooked up,
then in psychedelic song lyrics, skinny dipping, drugs.
(Who knew skateboarding stoned was so funny and

bizarre?) But the best he saved for last. He pilfered a
road flare from his parents' Cadillac, announced our
real adventure awaited us. He marched us down the
hill, along the rusted railroad tracks, until we arrived

at the tunnel mouth. Peering into the uneasy
darkness, we could just make out the far side, a tiny
green window at some impossible distance. He took
out a lighter from his pocket, sparked the road flare,

and sternly warned us: *Remember to watch your feet
on the ties, so you don't fall, and if the train comes,
for God's sake, press yourselves hard against the
tunnel wall.* None of us knew whether the train would

come or not, but when Paul vanished into the dark
mouth, we followed like his pack, hooting & barking
& screaming as we followed the red sparkling eye of
the flare into the abyss. For a long time, nothing

49

stirred but smoke and sparks, the sound of stumbling
footsteps and the hard ragged edge of breath. Then
Paul stopped dead, and we plowed into one another
like a burning freeway pileup. *Do you hear it coming?*

he whispered, pouring gasoline on the fire. Someone
screamed. In a panic, we madly sprinted toward the
opening on the far end. In the sheer terror of that
underworld, none of us knew whether a fire-breathing

train readied itself to mow us down or if he was just
pulling our leg. After the forever ended, we rushed out
into the sunlight, each of us yelping and screeching
we'd survived. Paul beamed as we shook off the

shadows. And only then, did I notice how the world
had somehow opened. For a moment, standing there,
chuffing from the hard run, sweat and ash still
burning my eyes, I felt that I had stepped out of the

tiny set of my life. In the blinding sunlight Paul had
dragged us into, it was as if every door were thrown
open and the old world was punctured, revealing what
remained as the real shadows, compared to this new

world in which even the leaves of the trees shone hard
and bright with a grace I seemed to have never known
before.

Abecedarian on the Cusp of Despair

About hope, I've almost had enough: every time this
nation shoves the burning dumpsters of itself closer
to the cliff's edge, some fool says, poetry is going to
save us! I seriously doubt it. We poets might raise the
torch of our fiery voices, igniting every chanting mob
to give witness to this nightmare. We might tilt our
faces to the crazy blue light of the polemic, but do you
honestly think some housewife in Peoria gives a damn
about poetry, is influenced one iota based on your
passionate villanelle? Finds hope in your airy stanzas
& meaningful metaphors? How about we let poetry be
what it is—this telling slant of lyricism setting watch
fires burning, that doesn't just flare up & fade, like
joss paper? Let's keep poetry for more important
matters: Let's decide language matters more than the
news cycle. That no deep change for us as a nation, no
fleeting opinion poll of verse, will turn the tiller hard
enough to correct our course. If people want verse to
metamorphose our nation, we're going to need
language that questions everywhere we have
foundered, resists the easy tendency to pick up the
compass and say we're so fucking lost. No, poetry is
just the tip of some unseen great blue iceberg
undergirding what we have ignored all along. You see
the true value of poetry is that it wakes us up to all
we've grown willfully blind to, even if it's the X right
in front of our noses yelling at us in our
somnambulistic death march. You want Zion?
You're going to have to let language awaken you
to everything.

Blood Necessity

My face is entirely forgettable, in the way
a tree is forgettable or a lawn, unless
of course, they belong to you, which
my face sometimes does. Sometimes

I find my face unfamiliar, like the color of rain
or frost-heaved rock shattered on the slope of a cliff.
Even I cannot say with certainty the color of my eyes.
Perhaps they are the walnut shade of earth before

the plow blade turns a furrow after the last frost.
Perhaps it is like what water does to the color
of chert, awakening a shade one cannot recognize
until water touches it. A beard, yes; a mustache,

undoubtedly; crooked teeth, yellowed
from too much coffee. A certain hardened
veneer to the skin, as if it had been dyed in decades
of too much labor, too much weather, a lack

of concern for skin care, or any sense of moderation.
It is a face that a thousand ships would happily sail by,
but not a sailor on deck might remember.
Only underneath the carapace of skin & bone is there

anything worth noticing. What words are there to
describe the gorgon's knot of language, history,
philosophy tangling the prefrontal cortex? What
image best describes the gossamer aesthetic

muscling heart and mind? Be honest—in this country, poets are invisible. They are abandoned to obscure bookshelves and people who pity them. Only when the first fires of the revolution are lit—or the plague

awakens—does anyone remember the blood necessity of what is otherwise so easily forgotten.

North Jetty

I have come to this edge for nothing. To write
a poem is such a useless effort. Even if the poem
amounts to something, what good will it do?

Will my sitting and scribbling this morning at the
mouth of Humboldt Bay, watching the indigo swells
roll in off the Pacific, change anything? Will it

for instance, feed a starving child? Or teach someone
to read, or cause someone to abandon a prejudice
poisonous enough to make them pick up a gun and

slaughter everyone in sight? Surely not. I kick my feet
against the concrete block where I sit, remembering
how my younger daughter one spring asked me to lift

her into our cherry tree, both of us burying our faces
in the white blossoms and laughing uproariously.
Until that moment, the blossoms had been merely

blossoms. It is the same with poetry, I imagine: the
poem seems to be saying nothing until a cormorant
lifts off, wingtips beating blue water—and steps into a

pocket of the air, disappearing westward.
As for me, I vanish from the empty beach, pocketing a
sand dollar as I go. When I set the circular form on my

porch rail and later fall into sleep, perhaps you might
notice how the full moon rises out of it, offers its pale
witness to everyone. Perhaps such symmetry awakens

our deeper longings, so beauty can master the real
work, transforming us all in moonlight.

Karaoke Bar

The angel in the silver dress ascends the stage
as if she were returning from heaven after a long
vacation with the seraphim. She steps to the
microphone, as if to catch God's ear, and sings the
opening bars of "Wannabe" by the Spice Girls. The
opening notes remind me of the sound of someone
strangling a cat, although to be honest, I have never
heard anyone doing that, and if I had, I would have
intervened. That is the problem: though everyone in
the room is wincing, no one here has the courage to
step up and say what she's doing isn't singing. Her
caterwaul expands as if she were expecting each sour
note were welcome. When she finishes, people politely
clap, I am certain more from relief that she's done
than to say, well done. Then one beer later, she's back,
this time promising "I Will Survive": but somehow it's
worse for round two. It's like the Wicked Witch's
nails gouging a chalkboard, like she'd swallowed a
frog that continues to croak, like a buzzsaw trying out
for choir. No, worse. It is the flavor of wincing,
Odysseus' request for wax in his ears. Afterwards,
I refuse to clap, but sure enough, another beer later,
she's steps to the microphone as if we have been
waiting only for her. I drain my beer and flee outside
where the rain is feathering the air. There in the
darkness there is only the song of a car going by, tires
whispering the rainfall's riffs. I sigh with relief, for the
evening knows the key and doesn't need to belt it out.
For now, it is enough to sing the blues slow and sure
and certain. And I am, humming along in harmony.

Poetry Is Not a Horse Race*

Poetry is not a horse race. It is not Shakespeare
twenty-five lengths ahead, trailed by Donne
Yeats, Stevens, Frost, and Whitman—and the rest
of the pack of dead white men whose hoofbeats
thunder in perfect iambic pentameter. Nor is it some
other pack of women or oppressed minorities or
whatever have you somewhere behind coming up fast
around the backside, moving like some amazing
machine to catch the leaders just before the photo
finish. No, the poet climbs astride her mount, clicks
her tongue or whispers some magic in the horse's ear
—and off they go. There is no track, nor other mounts.
She rides high into the mountains, having no sense
of where the journey will lead. Much later, when she
arrives, the horse will be blown, and the poet will
awaken into clear blue air, dismount, staring into the
great unknown distances. Don't bother asking about
the poem. Don't bother asking her about anything.
She has work to do that has nothing to do with horses,
or races, or you.

* "Poetry is not a horse race." Auden

On Reading My Name
in the Newspaper Mis-Spelled*

At birth, we are given our one true name: it is
both label and charm, an abracadabra by which
we are summoned. We bear it
as the most personal form of baggage, hoping
it will not be mangled into a nickname
or shamed by some bully or silly someone
who thinks the original needs improvement.
When it shines, we warm ourselves in its afterglow.
Offered in love, we blush or warm to the spell
of its call. But when someone offers the incantation
or praise—yet muddies it by mispronunciation
or mis-spelling—what then are we to say
but ouch?

*Dedicated to the local paper, which misspelled this
poet's name.

A Different Clock

"Grief keeps a different clock." Jackie Kay

Time lag stops the tick-waiting minutes, dragging
their broke-beaten heals. Everywhen, in every dust-

heavy corner, one cannot unnotice how a day
balloonfuls its enormous emptying,

like a chipful cup with a holeliness under it. Then
leadful, dreadful in their mud-slogged shoes

each longing minute wakewonders
at its frozen-self in the mirror-silver saying:

knows the broke-heart soul, there in its dustblanket
corner, weeps withend not. Weeps to world wake

the dead. Who, as knowful well, they must,
unwakeful sit in their own heaven corner

listening, listening, but telephone unringing, call
nowhen to us-living, misering out our endknot days.

Epithalamium

They say that for people who have never loved, love
poetry might as well be written in ancient Greek. I
would add, forget language, if it's written at all,
the words are some unbreakable code, for until I fell
into the gravity of the way you walked, until I heard
the mystery of your laugh, what the hell did I know
of love? Shall I tell you when I first saw this? Shall I
tell you in what season this wake-up call arrived?
During that trip to Portland, I recall you said, let's go
on, drive round the Olympic Peninsula in our aging
Volvo. Then when we got to the boonies, you, always
the adventurer, said, come on, let's get back off the
main road. I hesitantly agreed, scrying the sky, which
was nine months pregnant with the possibility
of an afternoon deluge. You drove, making a right
turn I said didn't seem right. You just laughed at me,
carrying us away on some dead-end spur. Rounding
the bend, you stopped, said, "Maybe you're right."
I was about to breathe a sigh of relief, but before I
could, you'd backed us into a ditch. Getting out, I
stood staring: the Volvo looked like the Titanic, tilting
hard toward its doom. All I could think of was what
my father would have done: how he would have let
loose in fury. I stood there, hesitating, breathing,
considering you. You said, maybe a vanload of
strapping young men will wander along and rescue us.
I stared at you as if you'd lost your mind. As my
mouth hung open, a white van shot past along the
main road. See, you said. Before I could respond,
the van backed up. A crew of young men leaped out,

miraculously pushed us out in less than a minute.
Afterwards in camp while the rain arrived in torrents,
you said how amazed you were I hadn't lost my
temper, didn't do what your father would have done.
Holding you shivering in my arms, I didn't say, yes,
that amazed me, too. When you stepped back, I only
looked at you, as the rain washed your face. After all,
you were by far the bigger miracle. Standing there in
silent witness of you, of your reckless courage, I
couldn't help but feel my heart surge in love and
wonder at the way you had driven us into disaster
—and called upon a miracle to save us, thinking such
marvels were as ordinary as the rain.

Crush

While I was muddling through college French,
there was this girl: blonde, petite, perfect
—a magnet of grace and intellect, realigning
my sense of gravity. I sat several seats behind her.
Watching. Waiting. All semester I listened
to her perfect pronunciations, the lilt of her voice
making words into magic. Her sense of style
rearranged the order of everything: her fine pearl-
colored blouses designer black jeans, those leather
boots, the way she bent all the light toward her when
she walked into the room. I thought if only I could tell
her how just the scent of her every Tuesday and
Thursday afternoon transformed my heart into a
raven: sitting on some remote redwood branch,
calling out into the emptiness, bringing treasures,
suffering for even a morsel of affection. I was not very
good at French to be honest. I didn't give it the time
required, only wanting to saunter the streets of
Montmarte, pen stories like Hemingway. One day I
decided French meant nothing: what mattered was
the courage to speak to her. During a break,
I followed her out of the classroom, down the hall,
to the elevator. When the doors sealed us into silence,
I summoned everything I had and asked her.
Predictably, she said no. She already lived with
someone: a professor, I recall. What happened after
that, well, we ossified in that tomb. Listening to the
sound of our stilled breath. The doors opened only
after all the oxygen was gone.

She disappeared, returning into her perfect life, and I pressed the down button back to hell, where I would rent a room for many seasons still, carving my initials into the walls. Thinking, mistakenly, my God, there is no place lower to go than this.

Based on a True Story

What they meant when they said the film
was based on a true story, or inspired by true events,

is that the director once had a distant cousin
who won twenty dollars on scratchers and gave half

of the winnings to his best friend to help him
settle a grocery debt he owed his mother.

In the film, the thread of two best friends remains, only
in this version, they are soldatos in the Mafia,

one of whom runs up a big gambling debt. The debt is
still a ten, only it comes with a hangover full of zeroes,

impossible for an ordinary crook to settle. His best
friend, a runner, steals the numbers to the crooked

lottery, sneaking them to his dear friend: with their
winnings, they pay off every dime.

The touching part of this gospel saga: the one with the
debt, well, his mother cooks up a celebratory dinner

of homemade pasta and meatballs. Just as she serves,
the mob boss shows up with five guys in dark suits and

machine guns. Tragic-but-true ending— the boys are
gunned down, leaving the mother splattered with

marinara and blood, weeping
as she bags up the leftovers. Based on a true story?

They rolled the truth like cannelloni,
so what's left?

Only the toothpick the capocrimine spits out
as he struts out the door laughing.

Slam

It follows you like some stray,
even while you yell at it, *Go home*!
It doesn't have a collar,
looks like the mange is eating it from the outside in.
You'd pitch a rock at it if you didn't feel a little sorry
for the damned thing.

You drag it home, give it a bath until the water runs
black as your soul, and the fleas are hopping
everywhere. You give it another bath. The drain fills
with so much shit, you have to get kitchen gloves
before you're going to so much as touch it.

It wanders out into the back yard and wails like a
banshee, like the dead who have come back looking
for the ones who killed their lovers or tortured their
families, hoping for a miracle to bring them back.
Your neighbors are yelling from the windows,
across the fences.

You'd muzzle the thing if you had a muzzle. Instead
you feed it and let it sleep on a blanket in the laundry
room.

Jesus, your partner says. *Are you out of your fucking
mind*?

And though you don't say it, you wonder if you are.
Before you were thinking, maybe you'd buy a cat. Cats
are, after all, poetic, aren't they?

You take the thing to the vet. It costs more than you
spent fixing your car last winter.

The Vet says, it has ringworm, something wrong
with its glands or liver or something, and the
medicine means you'll have to lay off the expensive
coffee for months.

Jesus, your partner says. *You are out of your fucking
mind, aren't you?*

And though you don't say it, you don't disagree. The
damn thing follows you everywhere. People who like
you or even love you wonder what's gotten into you.
You buy it a collar, as if claiming it. You struggle
coming up with a name.

You're thinking: Sonnet, Villanelle, Ghazal.
The mutt won't answer to any of them.
Won't give you the time of day.
Finally, your partner calls it Slam, as a kind of curse,
and the thing comes running.

You partner says, *Choose. The dog or me?*
Your boss says, *Don't ever bring that damned thing to
work. Ever.* Your family says, *It can stay in the yard
when you come over for dinner.* You don't even try to
take it into your favorite coffee shop.

You wonder if you're going to wind up homeless,
living in your car. One of those
burned-out remnants

you try not to look at with a sign
that reads, will work for beer.

Your partner moves out.
The dog sleeps on your bed.
Fleas and all.

You stay up half the night trying
to dream up something better
than the little you've got.
In the end, it's only Slam and you.

And if anyone asks, which they don't,
you practice your little speech, clever laugh
and all: you cannot even imagine
what life was like
before he followed you home.

VI

America Is Not a Racist Country*

Fortunately, Trayvon Martin was not shot to death
because he was black. Eric Garner was not
asphyxiated because he was black. Because he was
black had nothing to do with Daunte Wright's death.
Breonna Taylor didn't die in her bed,
shot by white police officers because she was black.
Thank goodness George Floyd lived in the America
we know and love where he was merely
being arrested, and that white knee on his neck for 9
minutes, 29 seconds had no connection whatsoever
with the color of his skin, even if the jury said
otherwise. If we cannot remember
the myriad of other names or situations, no matter:
we know without having to hear or read
that their deaths were merely anomalies. Imagine
that enslavement of blacks in America was just
a historical coincidence. Genocide against Native
Americans a fluke. No one here in the Land of the
Free, Home of the Brave would stoop so low as to hate
someone for the amount of melanin in their skin.
When people say America is a racist country,
they must be thinking of some other America,
not the one where the streets are paved in purple
mountains majesty, where it's always magic
hour—and everyone can get a loan or a job
or justice. You know, the country
where no black or brown person has to fear
for their life every time a cop pulls them over
for absolutely nothing. Where the bullets
do not prefer black bodies over the white

lies. After all, who would want to live
in that long slow
nightmare
of America?

*During the last week of April 2021, Republican
Senator Tim Scott, Vice President Kamala Harris,
Senator Lindsey Graham, and President Biden all
publicly agreed that "America is not a racist country."

April Fools

Not those who stood off
at some safe distance, guarding
themselves and you,

without saying so much
as a word. Not those
who stayed home.

Not those who bided their time
until they were invited
to have the miracle

of safety injected
into their arms. Only those
who said, it is our freedom

to do whatever the hell
we want when we want.
Unmasked, unvaccinated,

they barged in, as if they were
packing heat, asked for every freedom
in the till, robbed

the rest of us blind. Left a mess
of ignorance, which killed
so many for absolutely nothing.

Another Shark

The pool is enormous/ so big you cannot even see
where it ends/ it is full of bright blue waters/ the tang
of chlorine/ those lovely snapping aquamarine
reflections of light and shadow/ always the aroma of
suntan lotion in the air/ someone playing something
pleasantly familiar on the PA/ there are the joyful
shouts of children and the throaty cries of mothers
calling to their children/ the fathers throw their little
ones into the air/ and no one worries because even if
they fall they fall into water where the father could
scoop them up/ but they never drop them do they?/
yes everyone knows somewhere there are sharks/
everyone knows that/ somewhere one has gotten a
taste for blood or flesh but that's not here for god's
sake is it?/ not yet/ it hasn't happened to anyone we
know/ not yet/ of course there are sharks more often
now than there used to be/ they have sharper teeth/
they grow bigger/ and no one is doing anything to
stop them because it's a law after all isn't it? / but still
we all go to the pool/ we still spend the hours bobbing
and diving and laying out/ and no one ever screams
shark until a fin starts cutting the water/ we are so
used to hearing about this/ we know exactly what to
do/ we pick up a towel or a flipper and fight back/
duck and cover/ barricade/ run for shelter/ lock the
door/ climb in a closet/ pray as hard as we can/ text
the people we love/ only none of that works to stop a
shark does it?/ we wait for the police/ or someone
with a gun/ only that doesn't usually work either does
it?/ when the pool fills with teeth and blood/ some

send hopes and prayers/ the newspapers and the TVs and the electronic eyes come to spy on us/ and then go away/ and nothing is done because it is the law isn't it?/ until the next time nothing is done/ and the thing is we all know there are more sharks waiting for us in the deep end/ in the shallows/ every single day/ and no one can tell you anymore/ not really/ why the flag is flying half-mast today other than to say/ another shark right?

Connecting the Dots

Perhaps as a child, you loved to connect the dots:
how when you drew the lines, the shape of a dog
or a cat might emerge. Later

the patterns seemed to grow beyond imagination:
it took some effort to connect X to Y, in order to see a
lion or a dolphin hidden in that thicket. Who now

connects, for instance, the oceans warming
with the sunflower sea star die-off; or notices how
the purple sea urchins, with no predator to eat them,

ate the kelp forests, leaving only urchin barrens
behind? Or if not that picture, then who draws the line
between dying coral and forests consumed by bark

beetles when the frosts no longer form? Who connects
the slowing of the thermohaline cycle with the
diminishing of krill blooms—or how all life in the

ocean—and for that matter—all life on earth relies on
these tiny creatures? The way the tundra in Siberia is
melting, leaving sink holes collapsing in the landscape

and the organic matter that was frozen for millennia
now melting and off gassing methane, 20x more
potent than CO_2? Even if someone draws these lines,

their message is often buried in the louder message
that *everything is just fine, folks:*
keep on working, keep on consuming. That oil, gas,

coal extraction means nothing. It's business as usual while the lines draw themselves, and the planet is dying from all we've failed to connect right under our noses.

Goodbye, Ancient Friends

Sorry to say, but you'll never get to drink
at the Sunland Tree bar in South Africa:
someone had carved out its center,
so it seated 15. The ancient baobab died
just a few years back. All over Africa,
the same story is being told: the ancient baobabs

follow Sunland to the grave. On the island
of Socotra in the Indian Ocean the dragon blood trees,
battered by increasingly strong storms,
become scraps, eaten by goats.
In the White Mountains of eastern California,
a bristlecone pine tree named Methuselah, perhaps

the oldest living tree on the planet, offers no match
for two degrees of warming: a reality
coming whether we slow our emissions or not.
In that near future, all the bristlecones will die.
Say goodbye to these ancient friends—
and while you're at it,

see if you can explain
why we have
done nothing
for so long
to save them
or ourselves.

Just Maybe,

In the court room of white guilt, justice arrives late.
I admit this crime before I open my mouth. I offer my
privilege as evidence: I offer living a decade in poverty
after my father threw me out, having to join the army
to pay for school as some type of rationalization. But
it's clear how impossible it would have been if my skin
were black or brown. I am reminded how impossible
whites would have made such simple things as driving
a car or voting or getting a decent job. In the court
room of white guilt, I admit these advantages before I
even open my mouth. I have brought no lawyer nor any
words of defense for my race. How can anyone defend
the way we've treated you—how we enslaved you, raped
you, tore apart the families that we claimed you were
not capable of having. We denied you loans, we treated
you as if you were stupid, we made separate
everythings for anythings, as if even being near you
were too much; we burned your neighborhoods if you
got too successful; we jailed your son and fathers,
uncles and brothers until the neighborhoods
eviscerated anyone but mothers and sisters, aunts and
cousins left to try and show the boys some way
forward. In the court room of white guilt, I only say, the
sentence should be steep: let us pay back what we have
stolen, let us offer more than we have taken, let us
listen to all you have to say, and let us endure the
shame in the litany of wrongs we have done. Then,
much later, perhaps we can sit down at the table
together and break bread.
Just maybe,

Silences

Is there a way to say what must be said?
Is there a way to make the dead undead?

In the city that is no longer a city no one mourns.
No one comes to gather water or to share gossip.

No one reads the newspaper in the café.
The children don't play soccer in the street.

Still, in the forest, the naked girls hang
where the soldiers fixed them to the trees.

The mother who was raped and who had
her face and neck slashed must still nurse.

Only the dead remain where they fell:
their bodies in a row, hands tied behind

their backs, a bullet to the back of skull.
Now the soldiers take: first the children,

then the grain, then the machines to grow the grain.
They steal everything, as they stole before

until there is nothing left. No, not even tears.
And who would weep them, if not you?

There is no way to say what must be said.
There is no way to make the dead undead.

Tikkun Olam*

When this history is written, I wonder
where will our souls rest upon those pages.
Will it be that roused to march, we joined
that Wall of Moms, linked arms, and walked
right into a beating, tear gas, and rubber bullets?
Will it be that we joined the water protectors
and took our stand upon Backwater Bridge
that freezing winter night Sophia lost her arm?
Will it be that our sentence for pouring red paint
was life? Did we go to the concentration camps
to free the children? Did we bring food, clean clothes,
and a conscience? Did we raise our middle finger
at the passing limo? Did we run for office, saying
fuck you to the powers that would keep us silent
and stupid? Did we put down our phones, finally,
and get on with something more important than
ourselves? Did we feed the hungry? Help our
struggling neighbor, sing arias across the alley to
those sheltering in place? If the world is burning and
leaves are only ashes fluttering around us, and only
worse news seems to arrive daily on our doorstep,
when will the hour come when the spirit awakens us
to all that is undone and say, *Here I am!*

*Tikkun olam is Jewish spiritual practice of "world
repair."

VII

Master Class in Disaster

Pour water on the hot spots. Let the ashes settle.
Let the wounds scar over. Understand

what refuses understanding. Go to the boulder
in the field outside Philadelphia and ask, why him? Why

any of those people who just wanted to fly home? Stare
into windows and think of ice, salt, topaz: of her ruckled

face there, under the morphine, as she struggled to
breathe, the oxygen doing nothing as she began to cross

over, the lines ploughed deep into her flesh, the nurses
frowning in their hazmat suits, the monitor flatly stating

the truth. Gather with a few friends at that Italian
restaurant in Daytona Beach. Star says, where were you

that day? Imagine us all telling our mundane survivors'
tales. Only after we finish, Star tells us about her

nephew, his first day working at Amex in NYC. He had
those first day ticker tape skitters. When others arose to

go stand at the window, staring, he stayed glued to his
computer, typing diligently away. Only after the cop ran

into the room, shouted *it's time to go!* did he look up. He
raced with the crowd to the stairs, hurried down

with all the terrified sheep, dialing cell phones, trying
desperately to reach through the emptiness. He couldn't

think of anyone he should call. At the front door, the
fireman bellowed, *Whatever you do, don't look back!*

Gravity said otherwise. He remembered it in slomo: the
body hurtling toward him, the man's tie flapping

upward. He turned before the body froze him to that
spot. After that, none of us spoke. Ice, salt, topaz:

numbers mean nothing. It is the vacuum after the body
is lowered, after the ashes are cast upon the waters. Until

you have stood in that absence and felt love shattered
beyond repair, what words can offer explanation?

Ordinary Miracle

You are away in Texas. You went
to a dude ranch in some tiny town
with your sister, so you could make
her happy. You do that. You do that
with everyone I've ever seen you meet.
You spread happiness as if it were peanut
butter, as if it were your full-time gig
to crack open the broken places in people's
hearts and let the sunshine come pouring in.
You have cracked open my heart so many times
it is nothing left but fractures. And the sunlight
sneaking into the ache. Even when you yourself
fractured, and the surgeon had to cut out the tumor
and close up the nine-inch gap in your colon
and the doctors bathed your body for a year in
chemo—even then you didn't stop, though you could
barely stand. You gathered the lonely, the broken
women you knew and threw a party called the Wild
Women of the West Wingding, complete with plastic
cowgirls, plastic horses, plastic corral fences. You
played Patsy Cline "Crazy" and partied with those gals
as if it were the best birthday of their lives, and I don't
even remember what the party was for, other than for
the chance for you to love them as they couldn't quite
seem to love themselves. When Mary Jo died from
MS, you loved her right to the finish line—and then
you loved her beyond, named some hors d'oeuvre in
her honor we still love eating, so she will never die.
The thing is, I know you don't really believe in death,
not your mother's who left you at 13 when the cancer

undid her, not your daddy's who died just a couple of years back, which broke your heart into so many pieces that you seemed all tears—and sunlight streaming through. But I know it didn't stop you from believing in a place where death has no voting rights when it comes to the people you love. It hasn't even slowed you down, not even when you got a good paying job with two women for which the word "bitch" was given a special place in the dictionary. I watched you drag yourself home each day, beaten and bruised from the way they tried to make you less a miracle than you are. I tried to tell you to quit, but you weren't buying what I had to sell. And a month later, even though the other gal who works there can't wait to escape the toxic swamp, you turned their two bitter hearts as easily as if you were commanding the wind to fill their sails and blow them to a land where they could learn how to be human beings again.

The thing is, I didn't believe in miracles growing up. I didn't believe that the lame could walk, that the blind could see, that oceans could be parted or that the dead could rise up out of the earth and shake off their grave clothes and join us for drinks at 6. You taught me how to let go of that belief in what is practical. You taught me that love is bigger than all that, bigger than the broken self I look at in the mirror, the one I had learned to hate because, after all, isn't that the inheritance my parents offered me? You taught me that love is fluent in every language, knows where it is wanted, which is, after all, everywhere. I am just trying to say thank you, even though it took me so long to think of it, even though I have already said it

so often now I am afraid I have worn down the words
like the thinness of a beloved shirt or an old pair of
jeans. Still I am saying it. I am saying thank you
for helping me to become something so much
better than the thing I was when you washed
my feet so long ago in Alaska—and then rubbed
them with oil. It was such a beautiful thing to do
I didn't even understand it then. Maybe I still
don't understand it. Maybe I don't really understand
the miracle that you are, but I going to give it my
best shot. I am going to learn to love you
with the kind of love that forgets itself, like a dam
breaking itself open and letting the river go back
to where it belongs, and I will happily be that salmon
returning to you, leaping when the waters
form a wall, because
that is what a miracle is, isn't it?

.

The Secret of Poetry

Early fall couples with the ash and smoke from the
east. High in the Trinities and Sierras,

the fires erupt, walk across
granite peaks with fire tornadoes for legs.

Here the ash settles on us as if ready
to bury us. A friend sends an email saying

his group of poets has met and discovered the secret
of poetry. I go for a long walk until I leave everything

behind, until the sycamore leaves line the path,
umbering their reminders of a cold that can't come

soon enough. Much later at home I reread the email,
almost asking. Then I craft my reply. Even if they have

discovered this truth, I tell him, I am better off not
knowing. I am better off walking these empty woods,

uncovering the layers of duff with my imagination,
feeling where the mycelium is threading the earth, the

roots. Let the fires burn until they burn themselves
out. The heart, after all, bears its secrets too.

And some truths, though they rage white hot,
burn better left unknown.

Invitation

This summer I unravel like an old sweater, dithering,
asking questions that pile up unanswered. Finally, I

go sulk in my chair like a boy in a timeout under the
silken light of the cherry tree, missing the peace the

afternoon offers. Under that emerald canopy, I sit,
deaf, mute, wordless. Yet, somehow, I hear it: the

faint whirr and buzz before I see her: this blur of
motion streaking across the yard, disappearing like

river water in the leaves above my head. She chirps
down to me, saying something like a long-distance call

punctuated by static, but I listen, nonetheless. Later,
while I am grumbling through the dishes, she returns,

perching on the back side of the feeder where she
plays hide and seek, sipping the nectar. Between

drinks, she peers out at me, flashing her iridescent
fuchsia cowl and emerald body, as if in some code I

cannot decipher. Then, when certain I am hooked, she
leaps into the air, fast, faster almost than my eye can

follow—only my imagination keeping her pace, yet I
am reeled in, finally opening myself to possibility—

and when I do, I hear it like a struck bell, ringing,
echoing: the whole world whispering, come now:

everything, everyone is waiting,
and all the earth sings welcome.

Meditation on Approaching the Numinous

Do not go into the wilderness expecting anything.
Keep your eyes down, remembering what is wild
cannot be easily approached: Ask what you must ask,

but ask it slant. Listen to the sound of your breath, the
wind, the stream whispering over the cobbles, your
heart beating madly in your breast. Just beyond

flowers and stars, listen to what whispers beneath the
surface. What is it? Only, what always has been
spoken. Remember everything you so desire to ask

means nothing if you cannot just be still
—and hear this mystery give voice to all that must be
said, in a place where words mean nothing.

This Sacred Task

One morning camping along the Mattole, I rise in
darkness, hurrying past comfort of friends and coffee. I
rush northward, almost missing the rich greens and
tawny browns of the hills, the leaves awakening and

turning sol-ward to make their sugars, so every living
thing may flourish. When I rush onto the coast, the
road uncrooks itself along the black sand beach, a bank
of fog ahead, where the water growls at the shore.

At the bank's southern edge, a rainbow perches lightly
above the angry waters. I am so close to where the bow
touches, I could almost put my hand out, the way
children make a wing, and scoop out the indigo,

violet, blue where the colors flirt in the spindrift. Words
fails to describe what slows my hurry, stops my breath,
and I am stunned into silence. Later I try to recount
this moment to a circle of poets, dancers, healers,

helpers, but it's a wash: the photo I stopped to snap is
like showing someone a handful of ashes to stand in for
a house you once lived that flamed into memory.
In bed that night, I hold the moment again. Try to

understand. Listening, to the wind pass over the house
where I lie, whispering the answer to my simple
question, resolving like the passing of a suspended
chord. This is your sacred task: to remember,

to give it voice. How else will we save the earth,
or let it save us? Only in loving tenderness for our
witness. Only in asking what it means to be alive here
this day—to the terrifying beauty of this vast planet,

which, after all, is meant to awaken the answering
echoes of such terrifying beauty in ourselves.

First Farmers' Market After the Pandemic

After the great silence, we come
on this sunny Sunday to the plaza.
We stream onto the sidewalks quiet and contrite.
We listen to the wisdom of the farmers
as they tell us of the past year—how much fell sick
and died—how much had to be pruned back and
burned, if there was to be a harvest again. How long
has it been since we have seen so much bounty?
Children dance around us, laughing, but we speak in
whispers. One by one,
we arrive at the tables, take off our masks,
and receive
the snapdragons,
sage sticks,
homemade tamales,
BBQed oysters,
hot dogs,
and fresh baked bread.
We reach out our hands, stunned by the overflow
of cacti and sunflowers, infused oils and artichokes,
homemade tamales and sun ripened peaches.
We bow our heads before the woman who offers us
local mead, receive the communion of goat cheese
on a cracker with a dollop of jalapeno jelly, forgiving
us all of the ways we failed ourselves and one another.
And then, as if reborn, we find ourselves swept up
in all that is offered, we hug and offer back our own
blessing of laughter and tears, this unspoken
overflowing of joy after so much wandering alone in
the desert.

The Earthquake

The earthquake arrived just before Christmas
just as its twin arrived last year on the same damned
day, if you can believe that. If you can believe that,
then imagine how it hooked us up out of a dead sleep
and shook the house like an angry dog—
shook the wise men and Mary on the mantle off into
space where they plunged and shattered their fragile
hearts on the fireplace brick, shook loose piles of
books onto the floor, broke champagne flutes, and
shattered picture glass. That shaking seemed to go on
like a multiple-choice test on terror—
for which neither we nor the house
had studied. Only somehow, we all survived.
The next morning the power was dead,
the old bridge into Ferndale cracked,
houses just south of us jumped off their foundations
like pancakes flipped by toddlers.
People I knew shared their brokenness online,
showing us the shattered china, the broken bottles,
the ruins of the remains. I thought of
their loss, thought of the weight of it
like a lead basketball. Couldn't help,
but think of a friend I know who is dying
of a cancer that has memorized her middle name
and is willing to tell everyone just how much it hurts
as it tears her body down into its elements.
I thought of those Ukrainian mothers
whose children were stolen from them,
disappeared into Russia forever, or those who know
with certainty their sons or husbands are stone cold

dead from the bullet that memorized
where their hearts beat the blood into the body.
This is the way of the world, isn't it?
The way the universe comes to break our house
to smithereens at the same moment it offers someone
something far more terrible—strangles someone with
loss, drowns an infant in a swimming pool,
tips over a rush hour train carrying
everyone's loved ones home.
And God forbid you are the one
whose house didn't survive,
who gets to hear this impossible truth that someone
somewhere has it worse, which I suppose
is meant to lighten the weight of the lead basketball
but in truth only makes it more impossible
to pick the damned thing up. No, I'm telling you
the only way lifting it, of going on
is to let yourself be broken, let
your bones weep, let your loved one's body be buried,
even when it feels as if it's your own,
or you find yourself wishing it were your death
day instead. And maybe you go out into the darkness,
stand uncertain on the edge of the cliff,
ready to let the darkness swallow you: all I can tell you
is this: I cannot lift this terrible weight you bear in the
broken wreckage of your heart, I cannot bring back
your health, undo death nor loss. No one can.
But I will stand here with you. The two of us
can scream obscenities at the nothingness until
our lungs give out, until the tears groove our faces,
until after is a time that doesn't hurt quite so bad.
Until then, I will do what must be done. I will hold

you as long as you need without speaking—and then
even more, only because my heart beats too.
And this heart knows how to pick up
the pieces after the earthquake is over.
To get out the glue and fit the tiny fragments,
to throw away what no longer fits.
If this is the only way the world may be mended,
then I say yes to you. I will wait
until the wound mends, until the glue
can hold, until the grass begins
to grow in this place where we had mistakenly thought
darkness would have the final say.

Acknowledgments

"Accident" in *samfiftyfour*, Issue X.

"All That You Will Never Know" in *Synkroniciti,* Space Issue, Nov. 2023.

"America Is Not a Racist Country*" in *Shooter Magazine*, Issue 16, Jul. 4 2023.

"Another Shark in *Synkroniciti,* Haunting Issue, Dec. 2024

"Aubergine" *Sand Hills Literary Magazine,* Issue 45.

"Blood Necessity as Self-Portrait" first place in *Olivia's Desk* competition, Jan. 2024.

"Bord för En" in *Behind the Mask* poetry anthology, 2020.

"Chernobyl Spring" *34 Orchard,* Issue 5.

"Crush" in *Synkroniciti,* Space Issue, Nov. 2023.

"The Earthquake" in *Synkroniciti,* first place poem in Broken Issue, Sept. 2023.

"Epithalamium" in *Synkroniciti,* Family Issue, 2024.

"First Farmers Market After the Pandemic" in the *Northcoast Journal,* July 1, 2021.

"Hejira" (republished version of "Hiking to Hyperion") in *Campfire Stories: Redwood Coast*, 2025.

"Hiking the New Year" in the *Northcoast Journal,* January 24, 2024.

"Hiking to Hyperion" in *Synkroniciti,* Wild Issue, 2023.

"Just Maybe," in *Synkroniciti,* Vulnerable Issue, 2024.

"Klamath River Blessing" *Northcoast Journal*, Sept. 12, 2024.

"Lady Lazarus" in *Equinox*, Spring 2022.

"Meditation on Approaching the Numinous" in the *Northcoast Journal,* August 8, 2024.

"Ordinary Miracle: in *Synkroniciti,* Belonging Issue, 2024.

"Poetry Is Not a Horserace" in *California Best Emerging Poets*, Fall 2020, Z Publishing.

"Roadside Grave" won second place in the Dancing Poetry Festival, 2024.

"Seven Silences" aired on *Supernatural Park* podcast, August 2024.

"Slam" in *Synkroniciti,* Recovery Issue, 2025.

"Subjunctive Mood" *Contemporary Verse 2,* Issue 42.

"Superpower" in *Synkroniciti,* Family Issue, 2024.

"Three Mile Bridge, Late Summer, Headwaters" in *Parks & Points,* 2022.

"Tuluwat Island" in *The Eureka Times Standard,* 19 June 2021.

"Uncertainty" September 2020 in *The West Review*.

"Working within a Form" in *The Tule Review,* Oct. 2024.

THE AUTHOR

David Holper has published three earlier collections of poetry *Language Lessons: A Linguistic Hejira* (Deeper Magic Press), *The Bridge* (Sequoia Song Publications), *64 Questions* (March Street Press), as well as one novel, *The Church of the Very Last Chance* (Deeper Magic Press). His poems and stories have appeared in numerous literary journals and anthologies. He lives in Eureka, California, where he served as the City of Eureka's inaugural poet laureate from August 2019-August 2021. He loves that Eureka is far enough away from the madness of civilization that he can still hear the Canada geese calling. His website is www.davidholper.com

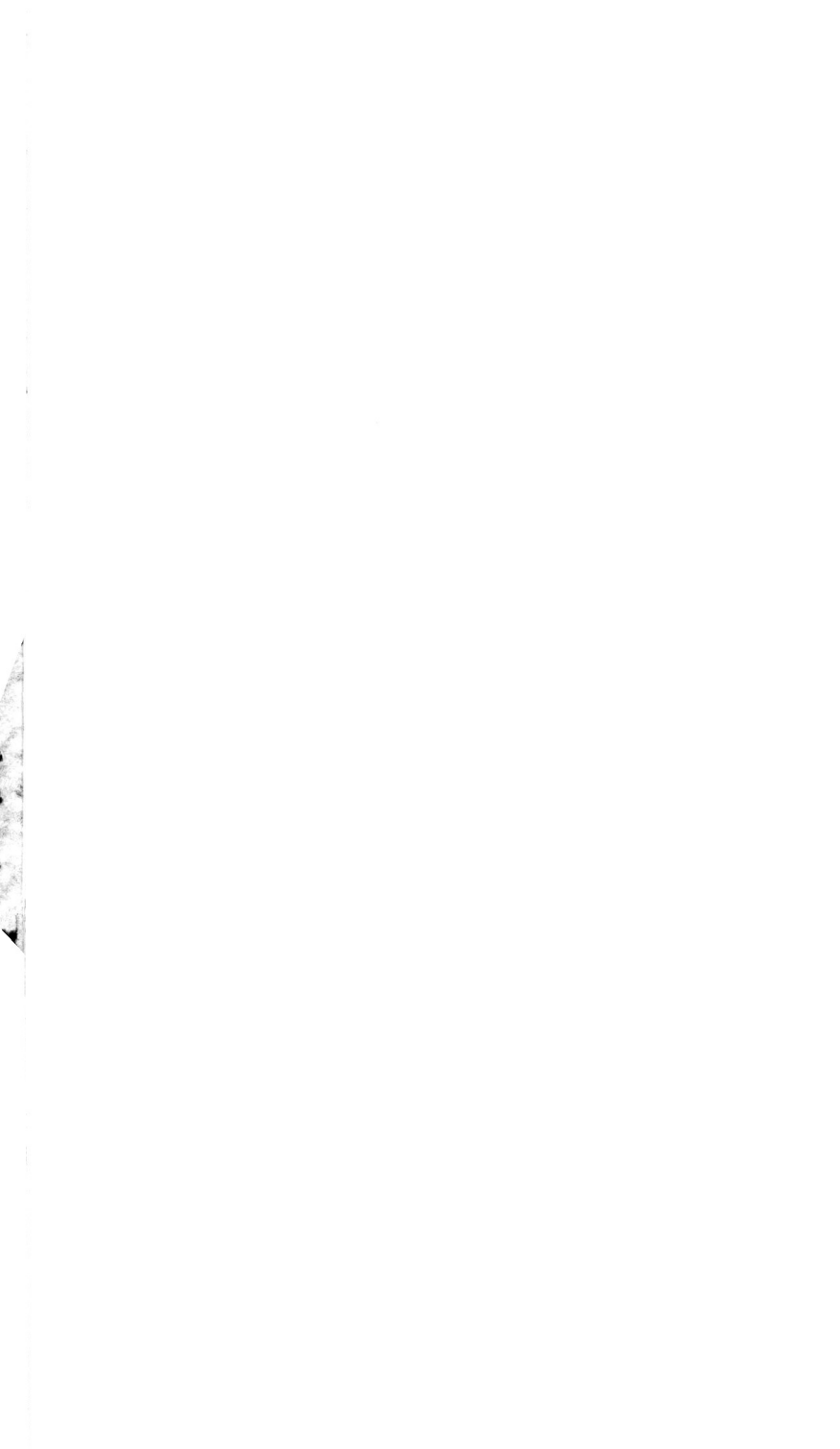